Sun Gazing

Aura Seeing & Naad Hearing

Exercises for

Psychic Seeing & Hearing

devaPriyaYoginï ~ Erinn Earth

Editor/Proofreader: **Michael Beloved**

Copyright ©2014---**Erinn Tanner**

Illustration on page 19, printed by courtesy of Editor

ISBN: 9780990372042

LCCN: 2015956104

Table of Contents

For the mystic within.

Introduction

The following information is offered from the author's perceptions developed through life experiences and the application of mystic yoga.

You are encouraged to apply the techniques for purposes of gaining spiritual insight and advancement rather than for increasing social status or economy.

In Sanskrit, supernatural powers are called 'siddhis'.

Siddhi literally means the attainment of a psychic power, the siddhi itself can become a distraction to continued development. Patanjali's Yoga Sutras lists eight standard expressions of siddhis. However, any successful accomplishment in psychic power should be used with discipline and insight.

Our goal is to observe these powers and self apply them, rather than direct their use for advantage over others. We make effort to avoid using the power to influence or manipulate material creation. Our participation in the history of the world keeps us bound to it. Our investment in it weights us down with consequences that may require the taking of more and more bodies. It is the responsibility of a yoga teacher to help others avoid this trap and to direct those powers toward spiritual progress.

Overview

Sometimes it's the subtle things we notice about ourselves that make all the difference in who we understand ourselves to be. I often ask myself and others questions like, "What is your relationship with yourself? Who are *you*? What is your relationship with the mind you use? Do you know that inside the mind there is equipment that causes thought? What is thought? What is the body? What is the mind? **Who am I in all of this**? Is there even an 'I' at all?"

Mother

When trying to figure ourselves out, we are innately compelled to look toward our own mother. For better or worse we often see ourselves as a product of our mother. However, when we consider the Earth as a whole we become aware that in the greater design of things our grandest mother is Mother Nature. There is so very much to observe in the environment she provides. Nature expresses herself in seemingly unlimited ways and in endless varieties of forms and experiences.

From the substance called light pouring out of the sun, to the structure of a tiny atom, we are surrounded by a material creation composed of both physical and subtle ingredients. When using normal consciousness we don't typically notice the subtle side of creation. As human beings our objective sensitivity toward psychic things is, on average, low. We have many physical distractions and interests. Yet, these fine elemental structures and equipments may be sensed and sometimes even seen - if only we could slow down and focus the mind in a different way. Making a practice of training the senses to see, hear and perceive things from a refined perspective might inspire an increased interest in matters of the soul.

Dreams – Living a Double Life

Do you believe that you are not only a physical being but also a psychic one? Even if you do not recall experiencing a single mystical thing in your life, consider that when you sleep, you dream. Dreams are not mere illusions or insignificant non-impacting events. If you've ever had a really profound dream, good or bad, you know it can affect the rest of your waking day. Some dreams affect the rest of your life.

Dreams are psychological events held in psychological environments. That is why we *feel* in them. We are still using a body in dreams. Dreams are events that should not be dismissed as imaginary mental creations anymore than this physical environment should also be dismissed as unreal. Dreams are evidence of our inter-dimensional existence; an existence that does not require the physical body's direct participation to be real. Dreams show us that we are capable of operating and associating in other dimensions using the subtle body.

Is it correct that you feel real in dreams just as you do in physical life? Is it correct that you are unaware that you are not using a physical body while dreaming? Even though we may not be aware we are dreaming, the psychological portion of ourselves still feels real. You don't think of yourself as imaginary in dreams do you? For most of us during dreaming, it doesn't even occur that we are dreaming because the subtle body doesn't make much distinction between this world and alternate dimensions. It knows it is real. It is used to going back and forth. It is comfortable existing alternately in both places. This shows that the subtle body doesn't require a physical one to operate. It actually lives quite the double lifestyle - one life in the physical and another in the astral during physical sleep – it is, in a way, like a split personality, one existence as the physical personality you are right now and another existence on its own in alternate dimensional places. Except for a vague intuition of one another, each side is often in the dark regarding the activities experienced on the other.

The dream world we spend so much time in deserves consideration. Since many dreams are astral experiences, as real as any experience in the physical world, they are an important reference point. We can look to them as a way of determining our level of consciousness. Dreams alert us as to the type of environments and situations the mind-body is compatible with, or, in other words, what energetic places we vibe with and are drawn into, psychically.

If you think yourself incapable of handling mysticism, understand that you already do. Do not disregard dreams. Indeed they are everyday mystic experiences that can provide incredible insight into an individual's existential condition. Besides, you handle them just fine practically every single night of your life. The dream world *is* the mystic world. None of us can avoid entering into it when physical sleep occurs. Sleep allows the mind to slip away from the physical body temporarily. The dreams we experience are a complimentary ticket into a supernatural environment, good or bad. Even though we still show up in these places as limited beings, we are forced to accept that the mind is designed for this back and forth living. We make no more effort to produce the involuntary experience that is dreaming, than we do to digest food or beat the heart. It's nature's way and even in the dream dimensions it is still Mother Nature's world.

My modest personal experiences with supernatural perception are enlivening, motivating and self-informative. They are a light at the end of life's mysterious tunnel of complication. They confirm that *what the physical body is designed to perceive under normal conditions, is not all that is.* The subtle world is all around us, infiltrating our physical bodies and operating them. Our bodies and minds are part of it.

Consider the sense organs. Note that they work on both sides of existence. I can see when I dream although my physical eyes are not operable. What eyes am I using there? I can hear, smell, taste and feel. I must have subtle senses. Although the senses operate on both sides, we note how they are similar. We also consider how they are different. On each side they operate to receive information in a certain way, either a very limited and coherent way, or an otherworldly, more incoherent way.

Coherent and Incoherent

In this world, within this atmosphere, our sense organs work 'coherently', meaning they bring information into the psyche in an orderly, chronological sequence. However, once the information is passed into the intellect only limited information is routed to the conscious mind, very little in proportion to what does not. The rest of the information goes to a memory bank for storage. On the flip side, when we enter into an astral environment, the senses may work in a more abstract, incoherent way. Some normal physical limitations may not be present. We may find that on the subtle side, without the physical density of the brain as a limiter, we take more in, thinker faster, easier and understand more. There have been times I have awakened from physical sleep only to remember that I had just been enjoying myself in an astral environment, at a dry erase board, performing advanced algebra. I understood easily *there* what I cannot *here*. It seemed so normal in the astral environment and it felt fun! Math has never been fun for me on the physical side.

This dichotomy is interesting and causes me to notice another phenomenon which is our perception of the sun. From the perspective of our senses, within the physical atmosphere, we experience the sun in an *incoherent* way. Meaning we see the light as being all spread out. We are close enough to the sun to be *inside* its rays, not outside of them. Therefore, when we look *outside* Earth's atmosphere, at other suns, (stars) we see them as coherent, pin-pointed, unified light. If we were very close to them, as we are our own sun, the light would be perceived as incoherent. Another example would be a streetlight. When you see a streetlight from far away, it looks defined. However when you get close to it, the light appears diffused.

It's all about position and perception equipment.

We work with endless dichotomies in this creation and beyond.

Existence is very complex.

Tuned In

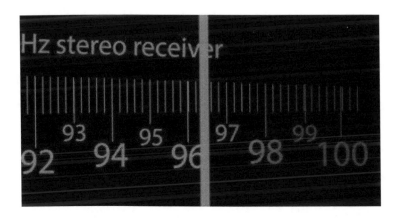

Nature has the senses set to a certain channel and just as when listening to one station you cannot hear the others, the senses are set to a limited frequency of information.

Under normal conditions the senses receive input from only a certain bandwidth of available information. We perceive this information as material reality, the world around us.

If the senses remain restricted within this narrow frequency, they perceive only what they are attuned to. Should that frequency be manipulated, resulting in a thinning of the barrier between stations, the perceiver may experience non local sights, sounds, smells, tastes or touches. These other realities are present right now, just as the other radio stations are, but are normally undetectable.

This booklet contains techniques that may help students develop focusing power, rainbow light perception, psychic vision and hearing. The instructions are simple enough for beginners yet fresh and progressive for advanced students.

Each chapter contains personal experiences in which I used a psychic sense organ. Some experiences were accidental, some deliberate. Included are exercises for enhancing subtle perception.

Summary of the Psychic Practices:

I focus on four (4) psychic practices.

1. Streamlining Interest Consciousness:

Interest consciousness is primary as it is a basis for the three other processes. Each technique depends on this underlying effort. If we fail to train ourselves to focus, we are bound to fall short and become frustrated. For most of us, developing subtle sensory perception relies on the willingness to slow down and become quiet and sensitive. This willingness comes from a spark of desire within to pay *special attention*. Paying attention can require much practice. It doesn't come easy. The mind has long developed its own ideas and established its own routine. By using the exercises, the nature of the mind can be shifted. Streamlining consciousness causes a withdrawal, or retraction, of interest from other mental activities. This interest energy is redirected toward full focus on a specific object or practice.

If the mind is thinking randomly, if it is stressed and distracted, focus cannot be appropriately given. This can cause a lagging, stagnant, easily interruptible practice session.

Using will power, we can apply full attention to the techniques, using abundant conscious energy for sensing out how psychic power moves in the head, in the body, and how one's *will* can influence the inward or outward flow of this attention power. It can be directed.

The great benefits of learning to streamline interest manifest in the reward of mental clarity, a high quality attention to detail and an increase in subtle sensitivity. The observing self gets a chance to see things through heightened sensual awareness like never before. This may cause a mental, emotional, physical and spiritual convergence – a togetherness of the self. This yoked being may experience brief or long lasting moments of tranquility. It is through this peacefulness that some of the wonders of creation might be perceived.

2. Sun Gazing:

These exercises do not involve staring directly at the sun but do require direct, unclouded sunlight. We will gaze toward direct sunlight using the eyelashes as tools of refraction. If there is trouble with the eyes not adjusting to the light, a thin blindfold can be used for gazing, allowing the eyes to adjust in time.

Mental and physical techniques are applied to streamline consciousness so that interest is fully invested in the gazing. By streamlining the mind into the light, we heighten psychic visual awareness, making way for the experience of super-natural things.

Although staring directly at the sun may be prescribed by others who study light, I have not found it beneficial. The few times I tested it, I only got a headache. I've pursued experimenting with light in many different ways, looking at it from different angles, playing with various eye manipulations, finally stumbling on a technique that allowed me to comfortably refract direct sunlight. This discovery provided me a surprisingly mystical glimpse into the glorious world of rainbows we live in.

The objective in sun-gazing is not to see how long we can stare at the sun, but rather to refract its light and study it.

3. Aura Seeing:

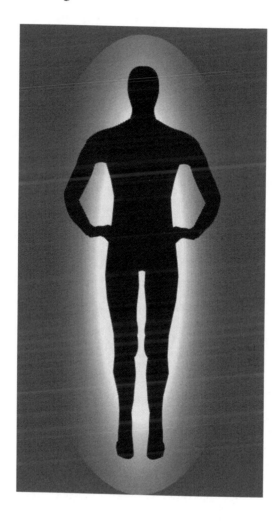

Everyone has an aura. Some people can see effulgence around the periphery of physical objects. In retrospect I find that my history of looking at and paying close attention to auras boosted my future confidence in the existence of the subtle body and helped refine what psychic vision I possess.

An aura is a glow of light cast from the subtle body itself. The aura is part of the subtle body in a similar way that lamp light is part of the burning filament within the bulb. Most of the subtle body's energy is interspaced within the physical form but part of it radiates just beyond it. What we perceive as physical is really a combination of physical matter and subtle energy. When a physical body is asleep or dead we see the result of the reduction or absence of subtle energies. The physical body depends on the subtle as its animating force. Without it, it is immobile or altogether lifeless.

The portion of the aura perceived as a glow around the periphery of a physical body or any physical object, is non-physical light cast outward, beyond the limits of the physical body. This glow can be seen with the eyes using special techniques involving physical and subtle maneuvers.

It is good to slow down and see another beings aura. It should remind us of the whole person, which includes, but is not limited to, the physical.

4. Naad Inner Sound Resonance Listening:

When things become very quiet in the environment around you, have you ever noticed a high pitched frequency in your ears, something like an electrical hum?

I have heard this hum in my head for as long as I can remember. It used to bother me at times. At other times, I found it mildly interesting. I did not value it as a special sound or as a means toward deep spiritual comfort. It was sort of annoyingly present, mysterious and often very loud. I would run a fan in my bedroom at night as white noise to subdue it.

We learn from yogic texts and direct experience that there is an uninterrupted supernatural sound frequency penetrating material creation. It is constant and unbroken. This sound is mentioned in the Uddhava Gita in a conversation between Krishna and Uddhava. During the conversation Lord Krishna said:

I am identified with the fine taste of water. Of the brilliant things, I am identified with the effulgence of the sun, moon, and stars. And I am the sound of the spiritual sky. *(11.34)*

In a translation and commentary, Michael Beloved explained:

Sri Krishna identified with the taste of drinking water, a taste that is greatly appreciated by many creatures. Of the brilliant things, He singled out the sun. He chose the effulgence of the sun, moon and stars. Of interest to yogis is the sound in the chit akasa, a sound heard in the vicinity of the right ear mostly.

This sound is used in dharana practice,

where the yogi links his attentive power to it. Sometimes a yogi is conveyed by this sound into the other atmosphere, the chit akasa. By listening to this sound, which is the un-expressed Om, a yogi attains kaivalyam, which is the separation of a spirit from its psychological equipments. By this he attains alone-ness, not one-ness as it is often misnamed. A yogi also attains spiritual perception by adhering to this sound since it causes the intellect to reach the drirah stage of quiescence.

There are those who hear naad, but don't like or understand it. On the physical side of life it may be perturbing, annoying, even traumatic. Naad can seem invasive when misunderstood or when it is approached with a lack of confidence and doubt. While it's true that hearing damage and other conditions can cause disturbing sounds in the ears, in many cases it may simply be an undiagnosed case of naad-sound-awareness. In modern society where we are offered a pill for anything, sure enough, there is medication available to subdue sounds in our heads.

Being uninformed about subtle phenomena, like naad, causes missed opportunities. It is good fortune to learn of naad, and then study it.

The goal of the three psychic exercises is increased subtle perception resulting in an enhanced and progressive spiritual practice.

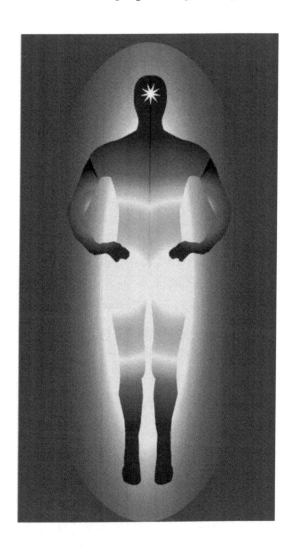

1
Discerning Reality

Let us first acknowledge the three aspects of our current reality. Much focus in yoga is devoted to discerning these parts:

1. The Physical Body

2. The Subtle Body

3. The Core-Self

Physical body:

Synonyms: physique, anatomy, biology, elemental body, gross form, flesh, mortal body, earth body.

A physical container of physical parts including water, bones, muscles, organs, blood, arteries and veins, wrapped in tissues, skin and hair.

Physical bodies are short lived. Even if a physical body lived a thousand years, it would still be a comparatively short life. Physical bodies are fragile and susceptible to illness. They are sensitive and adapted to living only on certain parts of Earth's surface. The body is a soft vehicle equipped with sensory devises that attract input from the outer physical world. But they don't last. We know this to be true because all physical bodies die. We cannot cite one that has not.

Some sort of physical body is needed and psychologically desired by entities (core-selves) within the universe. All humans, animals, trees, plants, rocks, everything animate or inanimate, are part of the force of material creation. This force organizes physical elements into an operating unit we use as the physical body.

The physical body is like a suit made of meat and tissue, it is basically grown by the subtle one in the uterus and beyond. On the other hand, the subtle body itself is also like a suit, but a suit made of mind energy. That mind suit animates and operates the denser physical suit until the physical one wears out and becomes inoperable.

Subtle Body:

Synonyms: psyche, astral body, energy body, dream body, light body, mental body, rainbow body, ghost.

The subtle form is another body. It is made of psychic matter. **It is not the soul, or spiritual self.**

We may assume that the subtle body began journeying through material creation at the beginning of universe. It is likely that the subtle body has lived through billions of years of conscious and unconscious development. It is likely to have evolved through various species, from one to another, and is now in human form. It developed a sense of self formed from all past life experiences and associations.

Although the subtle body is far more abstract than the physical one and requires special effort to sense, it is not formless or limitless. It is not undefined.

The subtle body is a container of psychic parts including; a psychological duplicate of the physical anatomy, the concentrated battery charge at the spine base (kundalini), gyrating energy centers (chakras), astral pipes and micro-pipes (nadis), sense orbs, and equipment inside the head that cause thought, as well as a sense of identity.

Think about that. Thoughts don't just happen on their own - there is equipment, made of psychic material, inside your mind space right now. These structures facilitate the phenomenon called thought.

There are specific types of thought caused by the equipment. Patanjali, author the Yoga Sutras, lists the five primary mental actions that occur in the subtle head as: correct perception, incorrect perception, imagination, sleep and memory. I have reordered them from most problematic to least based on my own experiences in meditation:

- Remembering
- Imagining
- Perceiving Correctly
- Perceiving Incorrectly

- Sleeping

The subtle body is adaptive and almost always desirous, ready for experience. It uses a physical body to fulfill desires on Earth. It seeks sensual fulfillment in astral regions when the physical body is absent. It does not die when the physical does. It continues to function on a psychological plane of creation. Between physical bodies it remains in a purely psychic form in a psychic environment, yet eventually becomes compelled to obtain another physical form. This compulsion is natural; a recycling function of nature called **reincarnation.**

The subtle body is inter-dimensional. While interspaced with a physical form it remains primarily Earth-bound. However, it partially leaves the physical during sleep, entering into astral dimensions it is compatible with. It is and will be the remaining psychological form when the physical one dies.

The subtle body is the target of a properly focused yoga practice. The goal of yoga is not an improved physique, but an upgrade in the quality of the subtle body and a clearing of its removable, undesirable contents such as heavy astral gases, detrimental karmic imprints and toxic energies. Left unchecked and unmanaged, the subtle body endlessly stockpiles memories and energies within its psychic parts as well as hoarding energies within physical structures like muscles, bones and organs. This causes the physical body to feel stiff, heavy and dull.

The astral form contains all of an individual's current and past life memories. Much of this is sub-conscious, thus unavailable to the conscious mind. It carries this information within itself because that is what it is designed to do. Over the course of time, a sense of identity develops which creates dependence. Attachment begins. This identity clings to the psychic contents, especially memories, and is doomed to oscillation between astral and physical dimensions, experiencing endless rounds of birth and death.

You may appear to yourself as if you exist in just one body. Other living things may appear to you, as one body. But for now the reality is that you are functioning as a collection of parts.

Think of a car. Even though a car appears as one object, we know that it is a collection of parts. These parts are combined into a compound structure we call a car. Special energies are required to bring the car to action otherwise it will not move. Infiltrating the car is an electrical system dependent on an igniting spark, a battery boost and a continuously available fuel. The physical body, being similar to the car, is actually wired with an elaborate electrical system that it depends on for its operation.

For experiences on Earth you need a physical form. To operate within the dimensional constructs of this universe, you must have a subtle body. You are not in control of this. You did not necessarily choose this for yourself. It is just the way it is. We might take heart in the assurance given by Lord Krishna to Arjuna in the Bhagavad Gita in which he explains that even he did not create the essence of material worlds – and that the potential for it has always existed.

Core-Self:

Synonyms: spirit, spiritual person, soul, atma, jiva, eternal person, objective self, observing self, divine being, self, living being, I am, conscious being, singularity, etc.

The core-self is a unit of spiritual existence, a living, limited, being, who resides within the central portion of the container that is the subtle mind space, in the middle of the physical head.

This is you, the eternal you, often unaware of itself. The core-self may not have access to all the memories of all the experiences it endured, but as aspirants of spiritual insight, we trust that within our individual psyche, they are all there.

In creation, there are innumerable existential units, you are only one. But you *are* one, so that is significant and important to accept.

You are not the physical body. You are also not the subtle body whose animating, energy certainly feels like life, but still isn't your own personal existence.

The location of your spiritual self can be sensed in the center of your head.

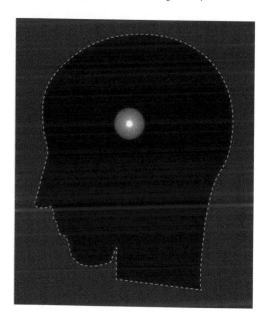

In this place we may sense a consolidation of identity, a convergence of self-aware, observant, consciousness; a consciousness that discovers itself as separate from the ever changing nature of the material world we are so powerfully intertwined with.

Inside the physical center of the head is an organ called the pineal gland. Physically it appears as a tiny, singular organ. Psychically, this simple gland is a kind of chamber. Within, an often neglected and avoided, spiritual person resides. The potency of the spiritual person is utilized by the body and mind for fulfillment of material and sensual desires.

In this text this spiritual person is often referred to as the core-self. This is the real and only you. You are the one whose being is formed of spiritual substance (anti-matter) and ultimately belongs to and is most content abiding within the spiritual world, in direct, uninterrupted relationship with God. Even though we are struggling with our attraction to material creation, we can again take refuge in the words of Lord Krishna once again. In Chapter fifteen of the Bhagavad Gita he says:

My partner is in the world of individualized conditioned beings. He is an eternal individual soul but he draws to himself the mundane senses of which the mind is the sixth detection devise.

The partner he speaks of is you, the real you - the core-self.

2
Streamlining Consciousness

The mind encompasses all that is mental and emotional. It desires a variety of experiences. This traditional wiring of the mind is the reason we crave art, music, travel, books, new lovers, new friends, new foods and new anything. Unpredictability is exciting for the mind, which, isn't solely about survival but is also very much about entertainment. When we understand the mind we can comprehend why television became so very popular so fast and the internet even faster. The internet is like a powerful drug for the intellect. Recently I saw a funny comic strip where the character begs the question, "If I get rid of my T.V. what will I point all my furniture at?"

Novelty is the very heartbeat of material life. Therefore, expecting the mind to slow down can be frustrating and may seem impossible. If you have tried in the past and failed you may have come to the conclusion that you just can't meditate. You may be right or you may be wrong. Only you can find out. Not everyone desires it. Every day we see that people die without fulfilling even their basic potential. They might develop a deadly addiction to drugs, alcohol or cigarettes, gambling, porn. Nature might squeeze every possible pleasure and pain out of the natural person until the body dies. Not everyone is done with the experiences to be had in this creation. That is ok. You and I are not cosmic police officers or astral judges going around arresting or punishing those who are in a different place in time. We needed our past experiences to get where we are now and none of us have perfect pasts.

Streamlining consciousness means engaging your will power to do the job of gathering attention energy from all over the body and mind, redirecting it toward the desired object of focus. The will power must do this over and over again. In yoga, this is the fifth stage, known in Sanskrit as '**pratyahara**', meaning sensual energy retraction. The core of one's personal will must insist that the body turn its interest away from external stimuli. The personal will must also insist that the mind abandon its normal programming in order to allow for a reversal of its attention energies. For most of us, this takes a lifetime (or more) of sustained practice.

If you come to a point in your life when you determine that what you want is to be able to consolidate your attention seriously, to not be scattered. If you believe that this will help you live a better life, even a spiritual life, you have a great challenge ahead of you. Even the greatest spiritual masters Earth has known have struggled with the overwhelming power the mind has to de-rail spiritual life. The mind is the ultimate, uncooperative partner especially in meditation. Despite spiritual aspirations, one's nature may get in the way. The desires of the body and mind are very different than those of the spirit. The more familiar we are with how the mind operates the better our chances at side stepping those distracting mental/emotional tendencies.

The will I speak of *is* that very inner spark of spiritual interest in something more than what is experienced materially. It is that spark of desire that we must build up, strengthen and make confident by these efforts. Eventually, the attitude of the mind may change. The yoga practice aims to reform the natural disposition of the physical and subtle bodies so that they shift over into an attitude of friendliness toward the spirit and of cooperation toward spiritual endeavors.

Practice has to be maintained. It builds up inspiration to finish the Earthly duties that spirit longs to put behind itself.

Mind = Senses = Lifestyle

Much of our focus in yoga is paid to understanding and reforming the mind. To control the mind means to control the senses. To bring the senses under control, lifestyle must be managed. The sense organs cannot be controlled unless they are regulated. Too much of anything can cause addiction. Sleep, food, drink, career, family, and socializing would need to be reevaluated and monitored closely. Decisions would be made based on what is best for physical, mental and spiritual wellbeing. Realistically, this means sacrifice.

The senses are placed by nature on the surface of the body. They are in direct contact with the external world. This makes them very important. The senses are profoundly influential and loaded with desire energy. They are exposed to so much during even just one single television commercial, one billboard, or participating in one conversation.

Daily Practice for Streamlining Consciousness:

1. Sitting upright but comfortable, center consciousness in the middle of the head.

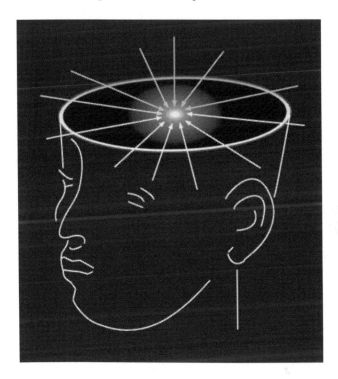

Sense a pulling power coming from inside this center, like a vortex. Sense this center as the location of your spiritual self. Sense that the self has a will to pull attention into its core.

2. Draw psychically from all of the 360 degree mind space, drawing that mental energy inward, into the middle of the head. Now draw from the sense organs too. Pull energy from the eyes, ears, nose, mouth and skin.

3. Pull from the whole body. Yoke the body to the center of the head, its interest energy released to the center of the head. Yoke the mind to the center of the head, its interest energies also released into the center of the headspace.

Core-Self Discovery DVD

Michael Beloved and I designed a meditation DVD that helps exercise the power of the will over psychic organs and their energies. The title of the DVD and its companion text is: *Core-Self Discovery.* It provides clear verbal guidance as well as 'mind maps' which provide simple visual reference to where energy in the head is being pulled from and where it is being directed to. These psychic exercises strengthen the will power of the individual. The will is engaged to gather the psychic energies from all of the five senses one by one. I recommend using this DVD or its companion text to aid in teaching yourself how to move the energies around in your head, instead of living lives in which the energies in the head are moving the self around. When the time comes and we are interested in spiritual goals, it takes major effort to turn the tables in favor of the self. By convention, nature is used to having the upper hand. If practice is ceased, nature will resume the upper hand once again. Remember this!

3
Sun Gazing

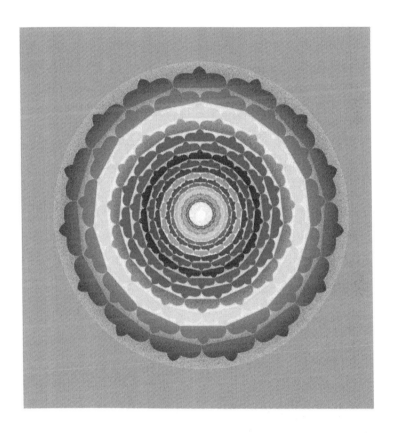

"To be able to see that everything is made of rainbows is a form of madness, but it is a true madness, and if you become passionately in love with rainbows then you'll see them dancing on everything. And you'll see pots of gold under

everyone, because people are all rainbows. The old story that there is a pot of gold under the rainbow is not just an old wives' tale, because if you've ever seen a rainbow that close and you go to the end of it and try and dig there to see where the pot of gold is, you won't find any ordinary gold, but you will learn something about rainbows, and that is that the closer you get to a rainbow, the more it will recede, because it's created out of your relationship with the sun; the angle that you have with respect to the raindrop and the sun's angle is what produces the rainbow in the sky. And this applies to everything. The angle at which you approach life will determine whether we see rainbows everywhere and in everything." (excerpt from Christopher Hills' *Nuclear Evolution)*

Sun-Induced Happiness

My conscious relationship with the sun started in a simple way when I was a child. Every year when summer finally came around in west central Illinois, I basked in its penetrating warmth, watching with my own eyes as it changed me from light skinned to brown. I couldn't seem to get enough of it. Not only was my skin changing, but as the closeness of the summer light entered the body, the mind also altered, my attitude shifted, I became more aware and alert. Life seemed crisper. I felt excitement, a sun induced happiness that escaped me during the other

Erinn and friend, 1987,
attempting to fry eggs on the hot street

seasons. Summer offered such intense daylight and lucky enough for me, the neighbor's swimming pool and a good friend. I believe that without the loving generosity of our across-the-street neighbors, who allowed my friend and I nearly unlimited access to their most awesome pool, my experience with the sun may have never been the same. Enjoying the gift of the hot sun, while also being able to cool off, was, for me, truly a magnificent blessing. My first days of studying light were during those wonderful summer days in Illinois.

The Sun's Hidden Secret

When a beam of sunlight passes through a crystal, we observe a new reality, a fuller, truer understanding of what light actually is.

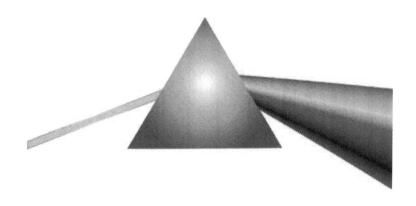

Nature designed the eyes to see only certain things in a certain way. They do not see everything. When the light beam passes through the crystal, we observe the rainbow light emerging; because of this we realize that, under normal conditions the eyes do not see everything. Light, a multi-layered material, is not simply a bright orange essence or a simple yellow dwarf circling the Earth. With the right perception equipment we witness that the sun is actually emitting a brilliant, seven tiered substance that includes bright purple colors, blues, greens, reds, oranges and yellows.

Nature's primary concern is survival. Upon contemplation of this survival instinct, we might determine that nature has good reason for evolving eyes that are not designed to see the full spectrum of light color. Nature may have practical purpose for narrowing our vision, causing a limited awareness of the environment.

Imagine if the eyes *were* designed to see the fullness of light. We might live in an incoherent sea of rainbows. That might sound nice, but on a practical level, life as we know it would cease to exist. Without the eyes organizing light, we might well live in a world of rainbows until night saved us from not being able to make heads or tails of our visual environment. Even the air would be filled with color. There would be little differentiation. But the eyes are *not* designed like this. They have evolved to select and consolidate light rather than filter and spread light. The eyes have physical and subtle mechanisms that differentiate, discern and detect dominant color qualities. This selective perception is what is presented to the observing self as relevant information regarding the external world.

Color observation is an important part of observing nature. Valuable insight can be gained when considering color in a meditative state.

The following chart is adapted from Dan Campbell's book, *Edgar Cayce's The Power of Color, Stones and Crystals*. This simple yet fascinating color chart expresses numerically the inconceivable vibratory movements demonstrated by the seven primary colors.

Color	Wavelength (angstrom units)	Frequency (vibrations per sec.)
Violet	4,000	750 Trillion
Indigo	4,200	700 Trillion
Blue	4,600	650 Trillion
Blue-green	5,000	600 Trillion
Green	5,400	550 Trillion
Yellow	5,800	520 Trillion
Orange	6,200	450 Trillion
Deep Red	7,000	430 Trillion
		*estimated

The chart is worth study and consideration. Contemplation of the numbers of vibrations per second at which matter moves to be seen as a particular color can be insight provoking.

Yet despite the fact that nature has the senses trained in a certain way to see certain things, we are not limited to seeing in only the normal way. We do have the capacity to use a different vision and to see beyond the normal means.

Discovery

I had an experience with color while in a swimming pool a few years ago. As I meandered in the shallow end, letting gentle water droplets play on my face and eyes, I noticed something spectacular. As I gazed straight ahead through my water logged eyelashes, with the sun shining directly down on them, brilliant colors appeared, danced, mixed and mutated. It was as if staring into a psychedelic rainbow kingdom. As I stared and studied the revelation before me, my vision shifted into an even deeper trance like state. The mind followed. I was astounded to see this new world of supernatural color right in front of my eyes. I felt as if it were somehow infiltrating deep parts of my mind. This was not what my eyes were used to seeing. As I continued observing, I figured that the eyelashes must be acting as a refractor. The presence of the water acted as an enhancer, super-magnifying the color. The sunlight was the substance being refracted and observed. Ultra rainbow drops, lines, circles, towers and spires of light, ultra-violets, reds and pinks, ultra oranges and yellows.

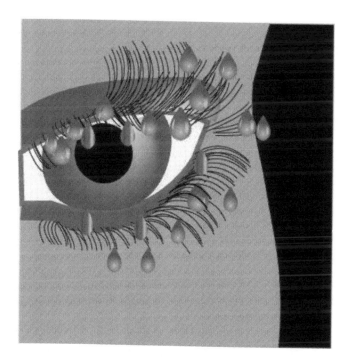

After the pool incident, I tried it without water, with just direct sunlight and the eyelashes. It worked. Although the extra water enhances the intensity of the color, it isn't necessary. For it is not the water but the lash, that is the refracting tool. Therefore all that is needed is the lashes and the light. Interestingly, mascara, a water based makeup product, also acts as a gentle enhancer.

I continue to study light. It is really the great phenomenon of the creation we live in. I once read that the ancient philosopher Plato said that, "Light is the shadow of God". Is it? Whether he did or didn't say it, it's a nice thing to contemplate.

What is it?

We are so used to being in it that we often fail to think about how special it is. How extraordinary. How does it factor into spiritual development? I've found that the more interested I am in the reality of what I am seeing, the more subtly focused I am, the more that is revealed to me. When I put down my mental agenda and release myself from resistance into a quiet, calm, mindless observation, the colors can become magnificent.

As I study the light, respect it and honor it with my interest, my eyes fill with a clean satisfaction and the core-self experiences a new feeling of fullness upon having observed a certain something closer to spiritual reality, than much of what it normally sees.

Exercise 1:

To prepare yourself for any of the psychic exercises in this book, you may find it beneficial to do some amount of stretching and breathing beforehand. Here are some examples of a few movements. Modify them to meet your specific needs.

A good release of built up tensions in the body and mind can make all the difference in the quality of your practice.

Breathe.

Perform a couple rounds of rapid breathing. Rapid breathing means to concentrate on the exhale by thrusting the breath out the nose just as you do when blowing it. Then, let the breath come back in through the nose but without pulling it in forcefully. Allow the inhale to come in naturally, as a reflex. Do rapid breathing for an amount of time you feel comfortable. As an alternative to rapid breathing, take several very deep breaths. Move heavy gases like carbon dioxide out of your body. Bring fresh air in. Physically and mentally spread the fresh oxygen around the body and mind.

- Sit in direct sunlight with your face pointed toward the sun. **Do not stare directly at the sun with your eyes fully open.** The eyes will need some minutes to adjust to the intensity of the sunlight. For now eyes can be either closed or partially closed.

The eyes may begin to water as they take in more and more light. They may continue to do this throughout the exercise or they may adjust. Observe this involuntary reaction.

Be comfortable and relax your body.

Quiet the mind and steady awareness within the center of the head.

In time, come into a state of inner equilibrium.

Your observational awareness is looking outward, from the head center.

Set aside all thoughts and concerns.

Feel the warm, direct sunlight making contact with your face, skin, fore head. Feel the warmth on your eyelids and lashes.

Notice the color of the light as it penetrates the eyelids and pupils.

Even though we are not staring wide eyed at the sun, continue to take plenty of time for the eyes to adjust to this. Facing direct sunlight means that an enormous amount of energy is moving through the eyelids and entering the psyche through the slight space between them.

The observing I-self is awake and alert, observant.

With the eyes cracked, eyelids dropped lazily, look at the eyelashes.

Adjust focus to look at the eyelashes.

You may have a sense that the eyes are turning inward. This is normal. Because you are looking at something so closely, the eyes may physically turn inward to centralize focus.

When this happens it may feel like the eyes are crossing and they are. This will not hurt your eyes. Stay relaxed about it, don't force anything, just be natural and try to get a look at your own lashes.

This is where the light is located that we are interested in viewing.

Adjust the angle of your head so that you can adjust the way the sunlight is passing through your eyelashes.

The eyes are looking for even small glimpses of rainbow light.

At once, we are focused, yet relaxed.

The eyes are likely reacting to the abundance of light.

They may tear up and involuntarily squeeze closed.

While dealing with the physical sensations, the mind may begin to feel like a whirlwind.

Watch the mind, don't let it whip you around, remain objective and observant with centralized consciousness in the middle of the head.

Study the light rays with a fresh perspective as if you are seeing it for the first time.

You may already see the light refraction, experiencing a world of rainbow light streaming directing to you, coming out of the sun, through what appears to be a short distance, onto your eyelashes and into your eyes.

You may see the sun's magnetic field which appears as thin cords of light energy emitted from the sun. These are coherent lines of light, bending as they reach outward. They may appear rainbow in color. This is a magnificent sight.

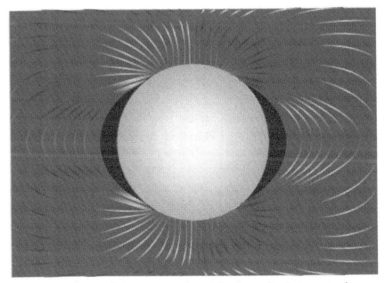

Mentally explore what you see, how the visuals change and move. Notice variations and color consistency.

If you do not yet notice the light refraction, adjust the angle at which you face the sun. Adjust the tilt of your head. Try to sense that the light is landing directly on the lashes. Be sure that you are in the open light and not in any shade at all.

As you continue to look, make slight movements with the head to micro-adjust the angle, attempt to make light that is passing over and through the lashes refract, revealing the spectrum of bright colors within the light.

If or when you see the rainbow spectrum, focus on it.

You will notice that it is never still, making it difficult to focus on any one color set or area.

Keep trying to zero in on one area or one drop and examine the spectrum.

Study it. Take in each hue.

Now, feel that you are pulling the light into the center of the head. Bring the brilliance of the color into the center of the head where it energizes the self.

Infuse the center of the head with the fullness of the experience of light in this dimension.

Identify and observe every one of the colors: red, orange, yellow, green, blue, indigo and violet.

Meditate on this light for as long as it remains comfortable and your interest remains in studying the light.

Exercise 2:

During the exercise take short breaks to rest eyes as needed.

Switch sides as needed.

Sitting in direct sunlight, turn the face 90° away from the sun, so that the sun is shining directly onto the left side of the face.

Close your right eye.

With your left eye, look to your right- look at the bridge of your own nose.

It will appear blurry at first, eventually focus may adjust.

Keep looking, use the vision you have.

This shifting of the eyes may seem unnatural but frequent practice will make it a normal feeling.

Try to focus in more clearly on the left side of your nose bridge.

Rest if necessary. Do not over strain the eyes.

Keep the frontal lobe of the brain relaxed.

Loosen up inner tensions.

Once you are able to focus in on the side of the nose, look closer and try to see the tiny hairs that cover the skin.

Most of the body is covered with a thin covering of tiny hairs. We are lucky to have these little hairs because they also act to refract sunlight. There are so many of them, each of them picking up and separating the light, causing the vision of what appears as an interwoven blanket of pastel light.

Look closer and observe the body itself absorbs that light.

Relax the eyes back to the center and close them.

When you are ready, turn your body around so that the sun is shining on the right side of your face now.

Close your left eye.

Let the right eye look to the left, to the bridge of the right side of the nose.

Stay relaxed of mind.

Keep the eyes focused but unstrained.

Again, look at the little hairs. See if you can visually sense out the light moving across the hairs, splitting into multiple colors.

Rest eyes back to the center, close them.

When ready, open the eyes, closing the left eye again.

With deepening focus power, look super closely, adjust the eyes and set your intention on attempting to see skin cells. Melanin within the cells acts as a solar panel while also refracting and absorbing the sun's light.

A soft, almost supernatural pastel garment of the same seven layer light spectrum may be revealed. This garment of light covers and feeds the body.

Focus on the light.

See what kind of detail your interest involvement can bring out.

This sight may appear like a blanket of interwoven cords of rainbow light spread all over the area of your body you are viewing.

Once you are able to see the hairs and the colors upon them, focus on the color to see it more and more clearly. Take the color into the center of the head space for examining.

The eyes become more passive now.

Deepen your singular focus, drawing in the supernatural qualities of what you observe. If your mind wanders, use will power to bring it back to the practice.

Feel that you are receiving nourishment, a revitalizing blast of light energy. Use will power to consciously pull in the potency of the highly charged colors you see.

Now begin to take vision in closer to the skin. If you take the time needed to allow the eyes to adjust, you may be able to see the skin this close up.

When you are able to see the translucent rainbow essence upon the skin, focus on it.

Once you are confident that you can stay in the zone of the light, let your gaze lightly explore the area of skin you can see.

Be aware that if you had the vision to see it, the whole body is actually shining with rainbow light. Not only is it shining with rainbow light, but your body actually consumes – or absorbs, light. You may even witness micro-droplets of light entering into your body. This is a wonderful thing to witness.

Relax your vision and close your eyes.

Take a deep breath in and out.

Move your eyes back and forth; stretch them side to side, up and down.

Now relax them until they feel normal once again.

Practice with a Blindfold

Some people's eyes are extra sensitive, making these exercises nearly impossible to endure. If you find this to be your situation use a blindfold for some days or weeks before starting the exercises that require direct light. The blindfold is not meant to block out the light completely but only partially.

The blindfold should be fairly thin to provide transparency. Make sure it fits securely and comfortably. Try a cotton fabric of light color and tie it around your head. Look toward the sun, adjust the blindfold to allow as much sunlight as you can tolerate.

Make sure you can still see the sun's rays.

The light should be able to penetrate the cotton, but also provide protection for sensitive eyes.

Adjust your head in a variety of ways, slowly, to test how the light appears when it is filtered by the blindfold.

Use the blindfold daily until the eyes become more tolerant of the light. People with lighter colored eyes may take longer to adjust. Some eyes may refuse to ever adjust, each person should find out how much the eyes are willing to cooperate.

Gaze with devotion. Consider at attitude of gratitude for the experience of sun gazing and whatever amount of peace and stability existing in your life that allows you the opportunity.

Continued Practice:

The purpose of these exercises is to increase subtle perception. The hope is that students will gain confidence in mystic abilities and use them for spiritual progress. We all have subtle bodies, therefore, whether we realize it or not, some aspect of every one of us is mystical.

Sun-gazing is a special practice that few people will take the time required to master. However, with consistency, insight will develop. You may notice and appreciate flashes of rainbows here and there. As perception deepens we see with new eyes, eyes with deeper vision; simple, supernatural vision.

In my own spiritual practice, I found that sun gazing deepened my relationship with the sun deity as well as Lord Shiva, the master of yogis. I created the rainbow graphic on the back cover of this book, first using actual paint and canvas, later using Adobe Illustrator. It was inspired by thoughts of Lord Siva during Sun Gazing. The sun is everything to us here as we exist on Earth. We are dependent on its nourishment and staying power.

Sun-gazing can be an act of devotion for any of us. No matter what or who we believe the sun to be, spending quality time with it can be spiritually rewarding.

It is my opinion that sun gazing can help burn away childish ways of thinking, increasing maturity.

Take the time to see what the sun is really made of!

To see the subtle type of color we study, your sense of sight will have to be refined, strengthened and directed. Your mind should stay calm and serene. It may take a little or much practice.

Do not become discouraged.

4
Aura Seeing

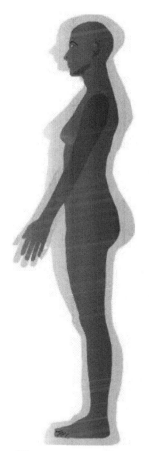

An aura is an effect, not a cause. Every atom, every molecule, every group of atoms and molecules –

however simple or complex, however large or small – tells the story of itself, its pattern, its purpose, through the vibrations which emanate from it. Colors are the perceptions of these vibrations by the human eye. As the souls of individuals travel through the realms of being, they shift and change their patterns as they use or abuse the opportunities presented to them. Thus at any time, in any world, a soul will give off through vibrations the story of itself and the condition in which is now exists. If another consciousness can apprehend those vibrations, and understand them, it will know the state of its fellow being, the plight he is in, or the progress he has made. (excerpt from Edgar Cayce's Auras booklet, Appendix I)

Sister's Aura

I was in the 3rd grade when I first took notice of a human aura. I wasn't very excited about it due to not knowing what it was and the fact that it bothered my eyes. The aura belonged to my teacher, Sister Georgiana, one of two nuns presiding over the Catholic School I attended.

Looking back, it's no surprise that Sister's aura was so pronounced. Despite our differences, I must admit she was a holy woman. She prayed and meditated. She was humble and devout. However, I found her ideas about the existence or non-existence of a soul within all beings offensive – she taught that only humans, not animals, possess a soul. This annoyed me greatly and I never managed to convince her otherwise. Had I known anything back then about reincarnation, we could have had a real debate.

Sister's was a strange aura. Despite not having much to compare it with at the time, it still seemed peculiar to my eyes. It was normal in its brightness and golden yellow color and that it surrounded her whole body, extending out about two or three feet. What was unusual was that the portion surrounding her head shot off like a wide beam of light, upward on her right. It was blank on the left side of her head area.

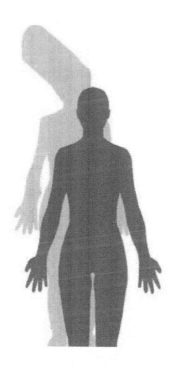

She spent a lot of time standing in front of a black chalkboard. The solid colored background accentuated the brightness of the aura. I spent a lot of time staring off into space. I stared straight ahead toward her, I didn't want to get called out for staring out the window, but my mind would go into a blank state of absolute boredom.

Tedious is the word, school was painfully tedious. I used to watch the clock tick so slowly. To this day my favorite time of day is 3pm, the hour of freedom, the time I was released into a world of activity again, talking, laughing, moving, breathing and thinking.

There was a limit on how many prayers I could memorize and recite to a classroom of fellow victims of monotony. Eventually a sort of depression and mental detachment would set in on the average day. The boredom and its resultant 'dumb stare' seemed key to my sudden perception of these lights around things and people. As I stared forward, my mind would slowly unravel itself; loosen its grip on the lesson. The eyes would droop a little, and begin to partially lose contact with the solid construct of objects before them. The usually defined outer perimeters of the physical body were no longer where the body ended. *In that altered state of consciousness appeared an additional figure, a form that moved along with the physical, but made of something subtle, something that looked like light.*

I am now aware that this subtle material is the periphery of the subtle form, like a skin. Most of the subtle form's energy is infused with the physical body, in a way masking its presence.

Brightness Contained

Most of the light is contained within the lamp shade.
But the light shines beyond the boundaries of the physical shade

Think of a lamp. We can't see the bulb because it is kept inside the lamp shade. Its super brightness contained. The majority of the bulb's power is within the shade. The light that radiates through the shade into the external environment is similar to an aura around a person or thing.

Not all of the subtle material contained in the subtle body can be or needs to be contained within the physical. Some of that material radiates beyond physical boundaries.

The most amazing part of seeing auras is that *everything* has an aura. When I get my eyes into a mode where I see one aura, within moments, the aura of every other object becomes visible! And I mean everything!

The doorframe has an aura; picture frames, plants and of course animals. Everything has an aura because every single thing, animate or inanimate has some amount of vibrant energy within in it. Everything.

Exercise:

To prepare yourself for any of the psychic exercises in this book, you may find it beneficial to do some amount of stretching and breathing beforehand. Here are some examples of a few movements. Modify them to meet your specific needs.

A good release of built up tensions in the body and mind can make all the difference in the quality of your practice experience.

Breathe.

Perform a couple rounds of rapid breathing. Rapid breathing means to concentrate on the exhale by thrusting the breath out the nose just as you do when blowing it. Then, let the breath come back in through the nose but without pulling it in forcefully. Allow the inhale to come in naturally, as a reflex. Do rapid breathing for an amount of time you feel comfortable. As an alternative to rapid breathing, take several very deep breaths. Move heavy gases like carbon dioxide out of your body. Bring fresh air in. Physically and mentally spread the fresh oxygen around the body and mind.

- Have a patient friend stand in front of a blank wall or door. If no one is available you can use another object such as a plant, a piece of fruit or a statue.

A blank white wall is recommended if available. If not, any solid color will do.

Be sure that the light in the room is natural sunlight and that any shadows cast against the wall are taken into account and not mistaken for an aura.

You as the seer should stand or sit about 10 feet or more away.

Get relaxed, physically and mentally. Settle down.

Empty your mind.

Fix your eyes straight ahead, staring blankly just over the person's right shoulder.

Forget that the person is there and just gaze. Don't worry about how long this might take. Anxiety makes it harder to see the aura because the mental interest is being used for something else, so relax.

Stare blankly above the shoulder.

Blink as needed.

There is no pressure to see the aura. Empty the mind.

Whether you already see the aura or not, abandon other mental interests or concerns.

Notice the vibration of energy active in your eyes right now.

As the eyes relax into a soft gaze, they may begin to move inward or cross. Your vision may blur or double. This is normal as the eyes shift from normal to abstract focus.

Be reminded that you, like everyone else, are a mystic being. At this moment you are trying see through psychic eyes.

The aura may look like a glow of yellow or white light around the person's body. Depending on the person, it will radiate outward between an inch or two from the body to several feet.

The aura may not appear even all the way around the periphery. Some parts may seem thicker. You may see bulges or indentions in the aura.

The aura may appear in colors other than golden yellow or white. Each seer sees uniquely.

If the aura became apparent to you, allow your gaze to settle upon it.

Work with your vision. The aura may appear, disappear and reappear. This is normal.

Keep readjusting the mind and experimenting with your vision.

Starting from the right shoulder, take your eyes up around the head, down to the other shoulder, and all the way down under the feet, up and around to the space above the right shoulder again.

As you move the eyes, you may lose focus of the aura. If so, start again with relaxing and looking over the right shoulder.

Periodically, take a break. Close your eyes. Take two deep breaths and rest a moment.

Open your eyes, gaze over the right shoulder again with a trance-like stare.

With eyes relaxed, keep gazing.

Using peripheral vision, notice other objects in the room.

Do they have a glow of light around them?

What shape does it take?

Can I discern between what is the aura of the object and other casts of light and shadow on the wall?

How far away from the physical object does the light shine?

If you still don't see an aura of any kind, don't be discouraged, instead, keep practicing.

As you gain experience, a mental and a visual adjustment is made. The eyes learn to switch over into another mode of seeing, from the everyday survival vision to mystic perception.

Just because someone has never put their car into 5th gear does not mean that 5th gear doesn't exist and won't function when applied. Similarly we may shift into an often unused mode of vision. We gaze off in a trance-like state so that the mind will shift to a heightened state of clarity and acceptance, a state where it doesn't have to be locked into normal sensory interpretation.

Continued Practice:

Once you have practiced for some time, you may notice that you can see auras even when you are not practicing. Auras may become more and more apparent. Take a look, but be discreet. Do not mention it to others, except to those who also practice.

Mystic practices are kept close to one's heart and soul and never used to impress others.

5
Naad Hearing

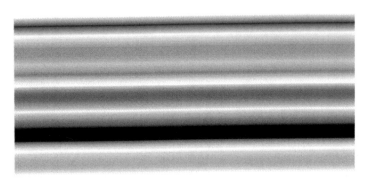

A yogi must dig deep into naad, become emerged into it, into its sound, into its vibratory energy. He should locate its node(s) and get as close as possible. He should note naad's blaring tones and its very subtle almost non-existent emittances.

The yogi should do this and should not be distracted. However, there will be distractions. A yogi must research to know why he was distracted. He should find methods of reducing the diversions to nil. The methods should be fool-proof. A yogi has everything to gain by becoming deeply absorbed in naad supernatural sound resonance. That will stabilize his meditation and eventually take him to the chit akash sky of consciousness.

(-excerpt from Michael Beloved's Kundalini Hatha Yoga Pradipika)

Common Sound ~ Common Listening

An ordinary sound comes and goes. We normally listen to such sounds with ordinary instinctual interest. Sound's vibration substance passes into our hearing equipment where the information is delivered to certain mental equipment. Keep in mind that the mind and its equipment surround the core-self on all sides. As the listener, the core-self is normally only made aware of sounds relevant to survival of the physical body. The mind performs an interpretation (or discernment) maneuver for each and every vibration that enters into its hearing organ. In a single moment the body can receive a sound wave, decipher the vibration package into sensible, relatable information and come to a conclusion which is presented to the core-self. The core-self may falsely believe that it has made this determination on its own, but it has not. It cannot be over-stated how important it is for the core-self to accept that it has little control over this process.

Think of the sound of each:

- Rain and thunder
- Squealing tires
- Laughter
- Firecrackers
- A cat's meow

These are material sounds, natural sounds, originating by cause of some action in our environment. They might trigger certain, possibly inconsequential memory flashes. These sounds travel as waves of subtle-material vibrating through the medium of air. If a hearing being is present the sound package enters into the ears and into special sound receivers. These receivers are designed to process and deliver these vibrations to the observer's organ of intellect which will then match them to related memory information. This elaborate process happens in a split second.

Uncommon Sound ~ Uncommon Listening

There is another kind of sound that we are not often familiar with. This sound can be mutually experienced by the physical and subtle ears. More importantly, however, is that it is of greatest interest to the *core-self*.

Yes! The observing inner-self experiences this special sound the most relevantly, most profoundly. Even more important than the other psychic skills combined, naad sound resonance takes us further. It is like a conveyor belt, picking up consciousness and allowing it to stream, stable and smooth, to the location of and eventual perception of, the spiritual self. Naad isn't really a subtle thing the way auras and rainbows are. Naad is something much more. Its results are not limited to insight into subtle material nature; rather, it offers a pure form of spiritual nourishment and energy. In my own experience, naad sound listening is the most valuable of supernatural practices.

Naad contains in itself, the power to take us closest to our spiritual goals. For some, that place is a heaven, a paradise of spiritual living. Others call this freedom **Samadhi.**

Transmigration ~ Samadhi

Evolution tumbles the seemingly ignorant living being through an endless series of births and deaths. Eventually the living being may take a *human* body. Within a human form there may exist a potential for the development of an independent awareness –a sense of individuality, or separation, from the physical body. If insight deepens further, the living being may also recognize a feeling of separateness from the abstract mental environment as well. There may be a feeling of, 'this is not my body' and/or 'this is not my mind'. The living being may begin to wonder about itself, possibly coming to believe that indeed it is a self, separate from the body mind complex. The individual may begin to study its self using meditation or another psychological discipline.

I would like to briefly touch upon the Sanskrit word "Samadhi". Common western usage tends toward defining it as 'enlightenment' or more ambiguously, 'oneness with the divine'. Samadhi is the eighth (8th) and final stage of traditional yoga. It means **complete insight.** This complete insight is achieved through efforts made in beginning and intermediate stages of yoga practice which are: moral restraints, recommended behaviors, body postures, breath infusion and sensual interest retraction. Body postures can be performed along with rapid breathing. This respiratory action causes an energy change out -

chemically in the physical body and psychically in the subtle body. Heavy gases are removed while fresh oxygen is infused. As one practices, self-interest is pulled inward and applied to the practice. This is called pratyahara, the fifth (5th) stage of yoga, meaning sensual interest retraction. It is the beginning step of yogic psychological restraint. While applying postures and breathing the mind is kept restrained, the wandering urges are effort-fully suppressed. These efforts prepare the body and mind as an environment useful for meditation. Interest energy retraction (pratyahara) prepares the living being for self reflection and eventually, in higher stages, divine association. Maintaining the foundational stages long term, may cause a step by step development of **objectivity** in meditation.

What does it mean to be objective? In this context it means to be independent from the influences of the mind and emotions. According to Patanjali, samadhi is the final progression in the three highest stages of yoga. In Sanskrit these three highest stages are collectively called samayama, meaning, complete restraint of the mind and emotions. **This is where samadhi begins.**

Complete insight (samadhi), is not just one thing. It depends on the person experiencing it. It has different levels and depths. It has beginning and ending stages. It is different for different people. Initial experiences of clear insight may happen for a single moment. These moments may lengthen in duration as practice progresses. It all depends on a person's level of advancement as well as basic spiritual status.

In the context of Patanjali's Yoga Sutras this blank insight, these gapping states of clarity in between mental functions, become themselves a means of perception. This clean, ('vritti-less') unconditioned insight is then used for study of various phenomena such as: time, language of all creatures, past lives, the mind and emotions of others, the solar system, the star system, the course of planets and stars, and the layout of the body. It is to my understanding that when highest samadhi is achieved, a whole new spiritual life begins. The self may experience states of consciousness completely outside the physical-psychic system that is material creation.

The samyama meditation sequence we apply in yoga is a spiritual conditioning program, readying the self for life in the spiritual world. Samadhi is when spiritual life really takes off. Of course, it is important to remember that just because one has attained a high level of spiritual insight, does not mean it is guaranteed to last. Maintaining this level of insight requires great resolution, power and sometimes divine favor. One of the keys to our success is our greatest friend in the here and now, naad sound resonance.

Back to Naad Sound Resonance

It is this psychic exercise that we take most seriously and spend the most time with. For the core self, this sound becomes a companion, the ultimate friendly hand to hold. One of the many benefits of listening to naad is that it rescues the core-self from the functions of the mind. (Again, Patanjali lists those functions as: remembering, imagining, perceiving correctly or incorrectly and sleeping.) Naad sound helps the meditator overcome these alluring activities of the mind.

Naad, the eternal word, is not temporary; it is causeless and continuous, without beginning or end. Even when you are not aware of it, it is still present. When one does become aware of it, it may suddenly seem like it won't go away. During the first part of my life, I certainly wasn't always comfortable with it, wasn't glad it was there. I often wished that silence was actually silent and not so strangely loud.

Quiet Life ~ Friendly Sound

I grew up in a quiet little town, in a quiet home, with quiet parents and one quiet sibling. Fate gave me the opportunity to experience much silence growing up. It was during these early years that I discovered silence to be anything but silent. Silence has a sound of its own. It *is* a sound of its own. When I first began hearing naad, much as when I first saw an aura, I had no idea what it was. Similarly, just as the aura bothered my eyes, naad sound bothered my ears.

As a kid I would ride my bike across town to the Catholic Church my family attended. I would go during the week or on a Saturday so the church would be empty of people. The church doors were unlocked and prayer candles flickered in the sanctuary. With high ceilings and beautiful stained glass, I felt the genuine pleasure of something divine flood my heart and head. The church didn't feel the same on Sundays when people were present. Alone, it was warm and welcoming. In this quiet, the sound of silence became unavoidable, a pleasurably magnetic, peaceful hum that seemed to be trying to draw me into a trance.

Holding On

I didn't understand what I was hearing or feeling in that church at the time, but the rich softness of the sound expanded inward and outward, filling both me and the building. I was afraid that if I let myself follow the sound too far, I might lose track of myself, so I would listen only for so long before cracking my eyes and breaking the spell. I had no idea about the nature of the mind so I kept a firm connection to my physical surroundings. I do sometimes wonder where I would have gone had I let go. Needless to say, I know now that, had I let go, no matter where I had gone, I would have returned to normal consciousness.

For this reason we should not fear meditation or naad listening. This so called 'normal consciousness' is actually quite tricky to get away from. The mind snaps back to normal consciousness naturally, as it is programmed to do. Even if awareness is able to momentarily shift away from normal function, finding itself in an alternate environment, you can be sure it will return to its normal, 'default' position, right back in the head, right back into common reality.

Family ~ Reincarnation

As a youngster I had some deep-seated issues that weighed on my mind and heart. I was an adopted kid. The relationship continuum with my ancestors was severed just after my birth. This would be a shock to any newborn's psyche as babies are very sensitive to the sounds, smells and vibrations of their mother long before birth. If you know even a little history on Catholic adoption practices in this century, you may know that due to my birth-mothers status - white, young, Catholic and unwed - her chances of leaving the hospital *with* her child were little to none. Under the influence of the church, at the moment of birth, I was removed from my mother's presence despite her objections. In these situations where babies were 'marked' for adoption, preventing even eye contact between mother and baby is strictly enforced. Within a week I was placed in a family unrelated and unknown to my birth families.

Many adoptees live lives as classified people, under contract to never know the identity, location, description, or history of their family of origin (unless the laws of the state change). Given a new identity and corresponding birth certificate, original birth records are sealed. I grew up blind to my past. I longed, just like anyone, to know where I came from and who I was. I had no story. For me, looking into the past was like turning around to see a blank wall. Sometimes I was angry at that wall. I would figuratively write negative things on it. My absent past was my greatest vulnerability. It was a reason for me to be hard on myself, to somehow be embarrassed of myself. We don't realize how reliant the psyche is on the genetic link for recognition of its own physical identity. Without this separation experience, one might never realize how dependent the eyes of the mind are upon seeing faces of those it resembles.

Spiritual Lineage

In a spiritual way, many of us have lost our lineage. While using these bodies and engrossed in family affairs, we drift further and further away from our source identity. Our higher relationship with the ultimate Mother and Father can go unnoticed. Ashrams, monasteries, yoga and other devotional practices, provide lifestyle control for purposes of awakening the living being in order that it redirects its interest toward culling out its spiritual origin. Other events have this redirecting effect too. Life experience, also known as the school of hard knocks, can force our awareness into altered dimensions of reality as well. Experiencing genetic isolation caused me to be sensitive toward a more subtle history of time and lineage. I literally didn't have a past to distract me from a broader reality. How could it be that the separation of mother and child, something so sensually sacred, could be motivation for a big step in growth? Could it be that the deeper purpose for me was the opportunity to study the nature of family, and this couldn't possibly be done without a special perspective derived from special circumstances involving great sacrifice? I think so. This is why today I am grateful to have had the experience. For studying the subtleties of familial energies revealed to me glimpses into the reality of reincarnation. These glimpses continue to develop into full blown insights. It is a rare point of view, a somewhat detached perspective. It is from here that I study this ever captivating phenomenon of nature.

Internalized Focus

The adoption experience also caused an inward turn. I internalized thoughts, questions, observations and loss energies. For years I was powerless with desire for information while at the same time feeling somehow unworthy of it. Since external information wasn't an option and therapy not offered, my mind did what minds do in such predicaments. The energy had to find somewhere to go and since I wasn't the type to 'act out', the only option was to go inward – and to my surprise I found something there! Within my mind and inner feelings was a surprisingly pleasant sensation of self and a feeling of security. The feeling was one of a higher existence that felt deeply pleasant. I questioned everything about my*self*. My psychic attitude was one of, "Well if I'm out here in the world on my own with no kin folk to be absorbed in, I will look and see what is inside of me and what is inside traditional families." In this life, they were a mystery to me.

Being separated genetically was like suddenly losing power and the TV goes off. The distraction becomes unavailable to the mind. The mind is compelled, only because it has no choice, to turn in on itself, to find something else to do. It begrudgingly must find what is in *it* that is novel, entertaining and fulfilling.

Part of my consciousness was given a great opportunity, but the cost was a brutal loss that had to occur as soon as I made my entrance into this body. But the gift was worth the ordeal. To contemplate family, reincarnation, attachment and loss; to seek association with the ultimate father and the ultimate mother has been worth the sacrifice. Time continues to grow within me the realization that I am not only this person or that person, daughter of him and her who belongs to this clan or that tribe. No. I am, we all are, something much more.

Devotional Listening

The intensity of the naad experience is not easy for everyone. Listening to a non-physical sound inside the head can seem like a strange project. The experience of the sound was harder when I didn't know what it was. I figured I must have an abnormality. I wondered why my senses were 'tuned' this way and why I had to be aware of this sound. It didn't seem as if anyone else heard it. At least no one mentioned it.

For the last 3 years I have been learning to sit and really listen. The reformation of my relationship with naad has occurred because of what I have absorbed from my teacher, Michael Beloved. Through his inSelf Yoga instruction I began to meditate on it, with it, consistently and with devotion. *Devotional listening* in meditation is so different than normal listening. Although I previously made an intellectual connection to what I heard in my head as being naad sound, I still had no practical understanding of how to integrate its divine qualities. inSelf Yoga teaches techniques for internalization of interest so that naad sound can be studied and experienced.

Description of NAAD Sound

Naad is like a hum, or an endless Om inside the inner ears and head. It can resonate with a high-pitched, full bodied electrical drone. When I was young and didn't know what it was, it sounded as if I was hearing the radio frequency of life itself. I thought it was the hum of silence but didn't take it seriously. In my ignorance, I had greatly underestimated the purpose of its presence. I was unaware of its higher qualities.

What I understand now is that the naad sound has always loved me, the core-self. It has always been a friendly presence whether I knew it consciously or not. It distracted me from mundane thoughts - shifting my awareness toward something mysterious. It is my job as a yoga student to love naad in return.

Before We Begin

As I am still a novice when it comes to serious naad study, I feel it important to include reference to an expert whose relationship with naad is advanced.

Please consider the following portion of the book, *Meditation Pictorial*, by Michael Beloved.

> *If one sits by the ocean there is a constant roaring, as wave after wave comes in. If one remains quiet*

within the mind space, after the senses are withdrawn from external interest, one will find that there is a constant sound within the being. This is the Naad or Nada sound. Yogis are particularly interested in this sound as it is perpetually expressed within and can be heard clearly and distinctly. It relieves one for the need of a mantra, so that one can focus within the psyche without props.

Sound

The sky or atmospheric space is the first dimension developed in the universe and the corresponding quality of sound developed thereafter. Sound is essential. In the beginning one will not see into the spiritual world visually. One will not touch persons in the spiritual world, or taste spiritual foods, or smell spiritual odors.

Flushes the mind

First one hears this sound on the inner side of the right ear. It is heard as a continuous blend of high-pitched frequencies. It is continuous without interruption and only if one breaks away from it by giving one's attention to the subtle or gross world, does one lose perception of it. This sound flushes

*the mind of random ideas, worries, troubles, and
lower associations of all sorts.*

A high-pitched frequency

*If one reaches a quiet place and then presses the
lower and upper right jaws together, one's focus
will shift to the right side of the head and one may
hear a high-pitched frequency for as long as one
can apply the pressure. As soon as the pressure is
eased and the jaw is relaxed, one may still hear this
tone.*

Relief from anxiety

*Once one learns to put the mind on this sound, one
can find it any time during the day or night. One
should meditate on it and get relief from anxiety.
This sound also occurs on the inner side of the left
ear but its frequency there is slightly different.
However, as soon as one reaches this sound, he will
find that his mind repeatedly tries to return to
mundane thoughts and gross objects. Thus one
might be drawn away from the listening practice to
become involved in mundane affairs.*

At that inner point

By careful study one can begin to understand that the spontaneous melody coming from the inner right ear, comes into the ear with a pulling vibration as if to pull the spark-like thinker through that sound into the spiritual environment while the sound entering the left ear has a slightly different melody and comes through the inner ear with a pushing vibration as if to hold the attention of the listener at that inner point.

A complex melody

If one listens to the right side, then to the left, then to the right, then to the left again, the sounds blend into a complex melody that fills the entire head. The sounds produced may twinkle melodiously into one blend.

Exercise:

To prepare yourself for any of the psychic exercises in this book, you may find it beneficial to do some amount of stretching and breathing beforehand. Here are some examples of a few movements. Modify them to meet your specific needs.

A good release of built up tensions in the body and mind can make all the difference in the quality of your practice experience.

Breathe.

Perform a couple rounds of rapid breathing. Rapid breathing means to concentrate on the exhale by thrusting the breath out the nose just as you do when blowing it. Then, let the breath come back in through the nose but without pulling it in forcefully.

Allow the inhale to come in naturally, as a reflex. Do rapid breathing for an amount of time you feel comfortable. As an alternative to rapid breathing, take several very deep breaths. Move heavy gases like carbon dioxide out of your body. Bring fresh air in. Physically and mentally spread the fresh oxygen around the body and mind.

- Find a private, quiet, out of the way location providing good ventilation. The meditation place should be indoors, if possible, away from even natural distractions such as birds chirping or road noise. It is important, especially as a beginner, that you find a *very quiet* environment, as silence is the easiest place to hear naad.

Center in the middle of your head, aware of yourself as the core-self with the mind surrounding you. There should be independent awareness, no mind chatter, no thoughts.

If you have learned breath infusion, practice three vigorous rounds of rapid breathing, studying the infusion of oxygen and extraction of carbon dioxide, into and out of the system. Detailed instructions of this special breathing technique can be found in my class manual, **Kundalini Yoga Home Practice.**

Sitting upright in your comfortable, preferred meditation posture, settle the body. Release resistances within it.

Settle your mind. Allow the frontal brain to relax. There should be no thoughts. Discourage the generation of ideas.

The body feels feather light. The heart is feather light, release anything within it. The inside of the head is feather light.

If you have a chime, singing bowl, gong or other tonal device, use it at this time. *You can also Om vocally if you have no devise.*

Listen intently to the sound.

Let it penetrate your ears.

Let it move around inside your head space.

As the devise becomes louder, keep the ears non-resistant to the sound.

No resistance in the head, hearing the ring of your instrument.

As you listen to the meditation tool, sense out a simultaneous ringing sound within the headspace.

This is naad sound resonance. The instrument can cause us to become aware of it.

Keep listening.

Hear the sounds from the location of the core-self.

Use the instrument for as long as you are comfortable, or as long as it takes to cause the core-self to become aware of naad.

As the sound of the tonal instrument begins to fade away, keep listening.

Link your observing consciousness to the remaining ringing within your head.

Listen intently.

Allow the sound to continue growing if it begins to increase.

Stay non-resistant.

Explore the sound you may hear.

The mind will attempt to bring core-self consciousness back into its interests; the core-self should pull itself out of the mental atmosphere and return to listening.

Exercise Tip: If you're having trouble:

If you are having trouble detecting naad, don't be discouraged. It isn't a sound we are used to hearing, much less valuing.

A silent environment helps immensely. Find a place of little to absolutely no sound.

Listen to the silence.

The silence itself has a sound, try to detect it.

Sense it out as a sort of open channel or frequency.

Regard the silence as a medium.

Listen to the silence, see what you hear.

If this helps you detect naad sound, take encouragement! Even if it still feels unnatural.

Link to this silence each time you come into meditation in order to find naad.

Once you are confident that you are hearing naad, spend time in your meditations with it. Develop a relationship with it. Allow its power to upgrade your physio-subtle-vibration by filling the entire mind container and all of its parts with spiritual sound energy.

Once you meditate with naad for some time you may find that your relationship with it evolved. Through practice and dedication, consistency and trust, one climbs to new levels of unfolding the spiritual destiny and identity.

Conclusion

I want to thank you for reading my book. It has come about as the third in a sequence of books I have written which are dedicated to providing education on mystic yoga. I thank you again if you practiced any of the exercises I offer here.

This book has been written out of a genuine appreciation for Mother Nature and the wonders of her material creation. Our mother's beauty and majesty can sometimes be overwhelming. Sensitive souls like my-self have come to understand that our ideas of right and wrong have little to do with mothers thinking. She thinks for herself. This makes her a force to be respected, never under-estimated and delicately handled - just like all mothers. Yet, however magical the secrets of her creation may seem, no matter how beautiful or barbaric her nature may be, there will always be those certain souls who long for more. There are always those children who dream of getting out of the house, into a new world. They also possess the confidence to actually think they can. These people are often called yogis, yoginis, rishis sages priests, priestesses, seekers and meditators. As we study mother's subtleties, she can no longer hide the way out, she can no longer insist on our continued cooperation with her limited ideas for our lives and behaviors.

This book is dedicated to those souls who know in their hearts of hearts, that without a doubt, there is life beyond this creation – and for those who know that that very place is the world where the grown-up spiritual entity belongs.

Om Shanti Shanti Shanti,

Om Peace Peace Peace.

For the whole world and every being in it, we again say:

Om Shanti Shanti Shanti, Om Peace Peace Peace.

Peace be with you! Namaste.

Index

About the Author

Erinn Earth (devaPriya Yogini) is a Yoga Educator. Yoga is an ancient science of introspection, psychological purification and ultimate, effortless togetherness with the Supreme Person through meditation.

After graduating from Quincy University in 1996 with a degree in Psychology, Erinn discovered Yoga as the greatest of humanities psychological studies. Practicing the 8 steps of yoga shed a bright light on the nature of existence and inspired a deeper understanding of her-self. As a means to this end, yoga continues to equip Erinn with mystic techniques (kriyas) which provide continuous, aggressive purification of the ever self-contaminating psyche, as well as healing relief to the physical body.

Erinn discovered that philosophical study of the Yoga Sutras, Bhagavad Gita and Hatha Yoga Pradipika, as well as yogic exercises, breathing and meditation caused a brilliant reform of consciousness- a much needed opportunity to sort her-self out.

Erinn was born in 1974 and grew up an adoptee in a rural Illinois Catholic family. She started singing and playing guitar as a child. She now lives in Sarasota Florida with her son.

Yoga teaching began in 2000 after formal training at the Sivananda Ashram in the Laurentian Mountains of Quebec. There, Erinn lived in a tent and studied with monks. She conscientiously engaged in yoga austerities, fully cooperative with the requirements of study and controlled lifestyle. This is where she learned the sacred discipline of Kirtan chanting that she shares with students and friends.

In 2013 Erinn met inSelf Yoga™ master, Michael Beloved, and received training in breath infusion for subtle body transformation, a form of kundalini hatha yoga. She has received two inSelf Yoga™ certifications and continues teaching under his guidance.

Publications

Core-Self Discovery

This guided meditation, narrated by devaPriya, is available on DVD and in book form for easy carry along.

This is the pictorial format of the inSelf Yoga˚ course for discovering the core-self in the psyche of the individual soul. This was adapted from Michael Beloved's "Meditation Pictorial" book.

The mind diagrams give graphic depiction of what should take place in the head of the subtle body during meditations for pin-pointing the core-self, the observing transcendental I-identity. If you do not have a teacher, then perhaps with this information you will not require one. This is book-guru. No need to run to a seminar here, a workshop there, a trip to exotic India or even a retreat in Colorado. At your leisure, anywhere anytime, this book-guru is available to you. Available online or by request:

Kundalini Yoga Home Practice

Erinn's fully illustrated booklet offers clarifying information on:

-Yoga's 8 Steps

-The nature of Kundalini

-Self-supervising a 5 part kundalini session for subtle body transformation including details on ' sensual interest retraction (Pratyahara)

-Advanced breath infusion (Bhastrika)

-Overcoming troublesome functions of mind

-Detecting the supernatural Naad sound as a source of concentration during meditation.

This book is a summary and an elaboration on the topics discussed in Erinn's group classes. Yoga classes can be opportunity for teachers to mystically transmit techniques to a few students at once. The student then takes the technique home and uses it to develop insight. Using the practice booklet as a reference for home practice, the student can then return to class prepared to receive another technique.

Online Resources

Website: *http://inselfyoga.net*

Forum: *http://inselfyoga.com*

Email: *devapriyayogini@gmail.com*

"It is very important that you get out of your own head, abandon your own ideas and **OBSERVE** what nature is doing.

Be realistic.
Stop Idealism."

- Michael Beloved

dp photoArt

62763511R00061

Made in the USA
Lexington, KY
17 April 2017